HUMAN 2.0

MAYO CLINIC PRESS KIDS

I would like to thank my father, Frank, for teaching me the art of journalism, writing, and finding difficult questions; my mother Emma, for being the single most positive and strongest person I have ever come across; and especially my stepfather Ian, who followed up an advert from the newspaper about a bionic arm. He started this entire journey, and I will always be grateful.

This book is dedicated to the family members and friends who have always allowed me to be myself, and always believed in what is possible. —P.K.

To my Wife, Huong "Bu," and my daughter, Dekye Dawa, both who have gifted me with a beautiful life. —S.R.

With gratitude to Sherilyn Driscoll, MD

MAYO CLINIC PRESS KIDS | An imprint of Mayo Clinic Press
200 First St. SW, Rochester, MN 55905
MCPress.MayoClinic.org

To stay informed about Mayo Clinic Press, please subscribe to our free e-newsletter at MCPress.MayoClinic.org/parenting or follow us on social media.

The medical information in this book is true and complete to the best of our knowledge. This book is intended as an informative guide for those wishing to learn more about health issues. It is not intended to replace, countermand or conflict with advice given to you by your own physician. The ultimate decision concerning your care should be made between you and your doctor. Information in this book is offered with no guarantees. The author and publisher disclaim all liability in connection with the use of this book. The views expressed are the author's personal views, and do not necessarily reflect the policy or position of Mayo Clinic.

For bulk sales contact Mayo Clinic at SpecialSalesMayoBooks@mayo.edu.

Proceeds from the sale of every book benefit important medical research and education at Mayo Clinic.

First American Edition 2025.

ISBN: 979-8-88770-192-9 (paperback) | 979-8-88770-287-2 (library binding) | 979-8-88770-193-6 (ebook) | 979-8-88770-288-9 (multiuser PDF) | 979-8-88770-289-6 (multiuser ePub)

Library of Congress Control Number: 2023057964. Library of Congress Cataloging-in-Publication Data is available upon request.

Printed and bound in China.

HUMAN 2.0

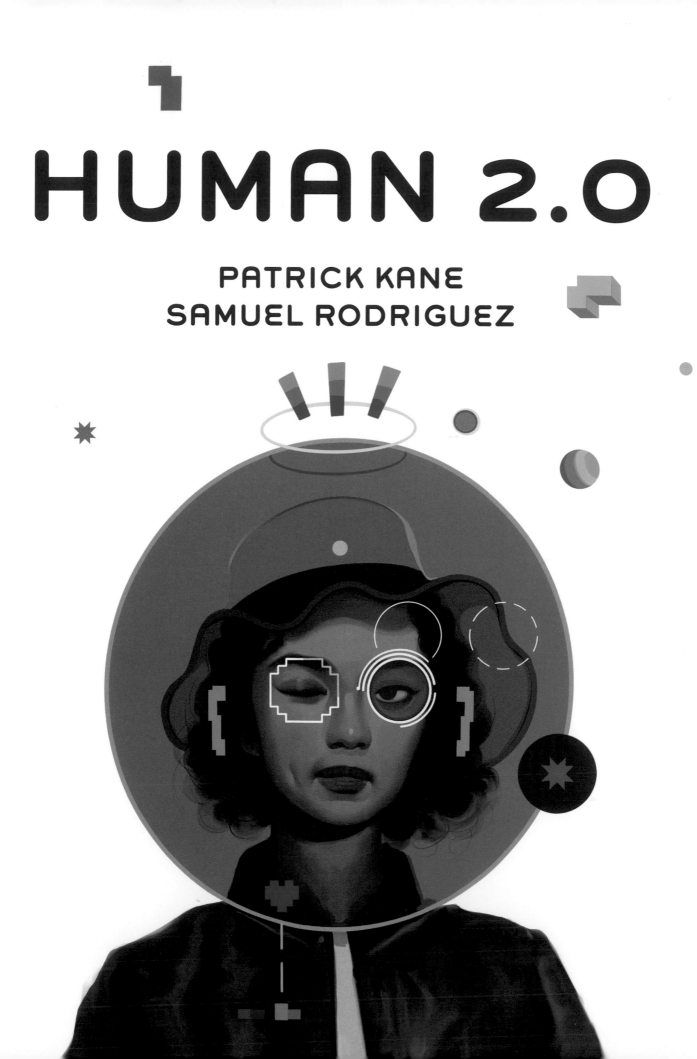

PATRICK KANE
SAMUEL RODRIGUEZ

CONTENTS

FOREWORD

In 1982, my lower legs suffered severe frostbite from a mountain climbing accident, and had to be amputated just below the knee. After the accident, I developed specialized prosthetic feet that enabled me to not only return to mountain climbing, but to climb at a more advanced level than I had achieved before the accident. Prosthetic feet with stiff toes made it possible to stand on small rock edges the width of a coin, and titanium spiked feet helped me to ascend vertical ice walls. From this experience, I realized that technology can rehabilitate, and in my own case, expand human potential beyond natural ability. These realizations convinced me to pursue a career in science and engineering so that I might be in a position to advance bionic technology, and to improve the quality of life for persons suffering unwanted limitations.

Today I am a professor at MIT where I co-direct the K. Lisa Yang Center for Bionics. The Center is now transforming prostheses from the passive devices of the past to brain-controlled robotics of the future. The most advanced of these systems have two-way communications, providing a person such as myself the ability to control their prosthesis through thought, and to experience natural touch and movement sensations when the synthetic prosthesis is touched and moved. Recent evidence suggests that such a two-way communication allows a person to experience their prosthesis as part of their body, blurring what is biological and what is not, and what is human and what is not. This is the age of Human 2.0.

Human 2.0 by Patrick Kane chronicles this new age. The book describes the body's journey through history following a technological trend in which bionic innovation continually expands human capability. The limit of this trend points toward a future world in which the body is no longer viewed as inflexible, but as a malleable design medium, able to be transformed at will; a future in which each person no longer has to suffer from unwanted limitations, but can freely choose the functionality of their own body and mind. It is my hope that *Human 2.0* will educate and inspire the next generation of young scientists, inventors, and technologists to continue the body's rich narrative of continual adaptation.

Hugh Herr

**Professor of Media Arts and Sciences at the
Massachusetts Institute of Technology (MIT) Media Lab**

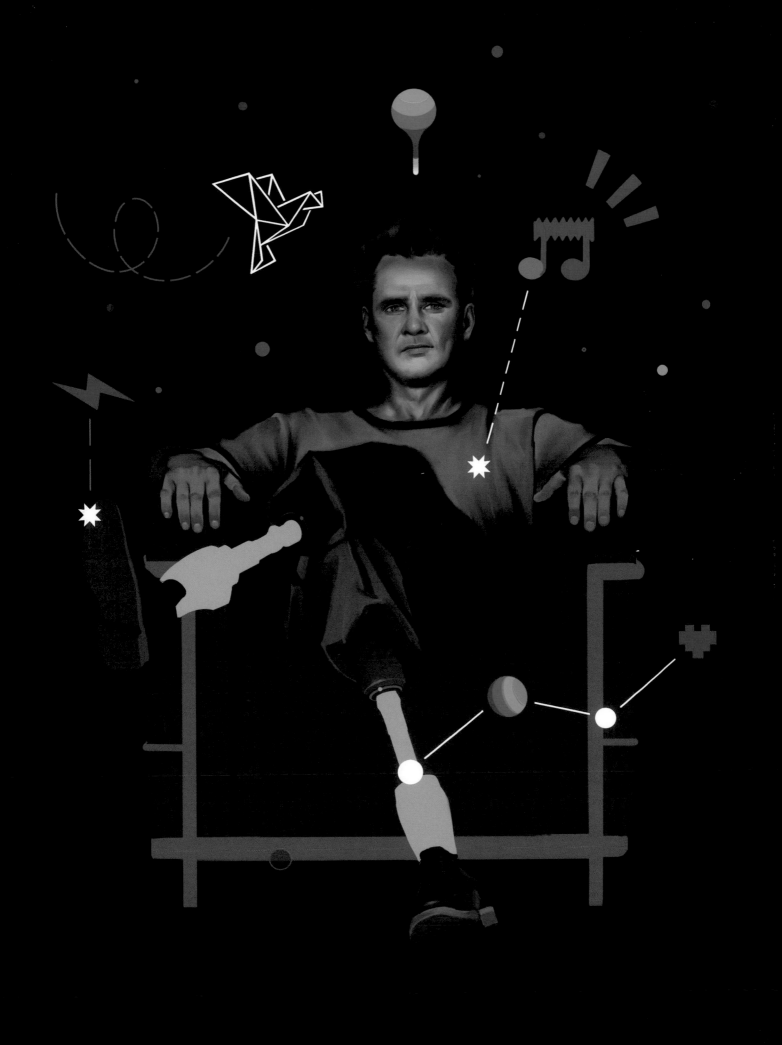

INTRODUCTION

Imagine a world where all around us are people with bionic limbs, machine-assisted hearts, and cameras for eyes. This same world has cyborgs who can hear colors and communicate via their teeth, and even people who use robotic skeletons to walk marathons. In this world, children learn to hear with external ears, and people born without legs can walk using ones made of metal and carbon fiber. Some people use chips inside their bodies to get into their offices, or to pay for their coffees on their way into work. This world is full of incredible people who are using technology to do amazing things...but the most astounding part of it all is that this world is the one we already live in.

Technology has changed all of our lives, and not just with the smartphones or tablets that we use. For some people, particularly those with disabilities, recent technological advances have crossed the realms of the purely imaginable, and reached a place of possibility. We don't notice it all the time, but bionic technology exists and is right in front of our noses. Far from a scene from a science-fiction film, the future is in fact already here.

This book explores the most recent devices that mimic biology, from intricate bionic hands (see pages 32–33) to neural implants (pages 40–41), and includes some of the major milestones that got us here. We will also look forward at the exciting inventions that lie around the corner, as well as what they mean for us as a species. Our journey to the future has already begun, and it is time to get to know Human 2.0.

THE FIRST PROSTHESES

For as long as humans have been around, we have been losing limbs, or are born without them. Whether due to an injury or congenital impairment (a condition that is present from birth), people have been trying to replace missing arms, legs, fingers, and toes for thousands of years. Early prostheses were revolutionary for their time, yet their inventors did not have the technology needed to provide better functionality and comfort. Even so, some of these early prostheses closely resemble those that exist today.

The earliest-known example of a prosthesis (an artificial body part) belonged to an Egyptian noblewoman almost 3,500 years ago. This wooden prosthesis replaced the big toe on her right foot, and even had a ridge in the shape of a nail carved into it to make it appear more realistic. It would have been strapped onto her foot with string, and scientists believe that it would have greatly aided her balance.

The earliest-written mention of a prosthesis dates to around 77 CE, and describes the iron hand belonging to the Roman general Marcus Sergius. Sergius was said to be one of the finest generals of his time, especially because of his bravery in battle. Across two campaigns he was wounded 23 times, resulting in the loss of his right hand. Sergius's replacement hand was strapped to his arm, perhaps allowing him to hold a shield for future battles.

Count Götz von Berlichingen

Perhaps the most famous example of an early prosthesis is that belonging to the German knight, Count Götz von Berlichingen, who lost his hand during battle in the early 1500s. Undeterred, Count Götz asked local craftsmen to create an iron hand with digits (fingers and thumbs) that could lock into place, so he could hold a horse's reins or a weapon. His love for warfare became so famous that some people believe it inspired the phrase, "to rule with an iron fist."

WHAT IS BIONIC?

Bionic refers to the transfer of technology between artificial objects and living organisms. The word itself comes from a combination of the Greek word for "life," *bios*, and the word "electronics." It was coined by American doctor and ex-US Air Force colonel Jack E. Steele in the 1950s.

Prior to Steele, the American biophysicist Otto Schmitt developed the concept of "biomimetics"—the transfer of ideas from biology to technology. In 1960, Steele presented an ambitious lecture and organized a gathering of experts on the topic of how new technologies could be discovered by looking at examples in nature. This field of research is known as biomimicry. A few of the best inventions to come from this field include streamlined swimsuits inspired by the structure of shark's skin, Velcro® fasteners modeled on how burrs (plant seeds) latch on to animal fur, and the shape of airplanes, which were designed by looking at how birds soar through the air.

Steele's lecture was titled *How Do We Get There?*, and the term "bionic" was later picked up by the writer Martin Caidin in his 1972 novel, *Cyborg.* From this point onward, the word "bionic" became part of today's culture and has been used to describe a whole range of prosthetic devices ever since.

BIONIC LIMBS AND IMPLANTABLE DEVICES

A prosthesis can be internal or external to the body. The ways in which people can replace parts of their body can largely be broken down into two groups: bionic limbs and implantable devices.

Bionic limbs are artificial body parts, which are intended to replace the function of a human body part, such as an arm or a leg. These are attached to the body, usually via a belt, strap, or socket, and can be easily taken on and off by their wearer.

"Implantable device" is a broad term describing anything that is surgically implanted inside the body. Because surgery is required to gain access, these devices cannot easily be removed, and are typically designed to stay inside the body forever. Examples of these include pacemakers and cochlear implants.

If either a bionic limb or an implant has batteries that need to be charged, they are called "active." Those that do not are called "passive." Some implants, such as cochlear implants, need batteries. These sit outside the body and attach to the implant via a wire, so the user does not need surgery every time the battery runs out (see pages 28–29).

A BRIEF HISTORY OF IMPLANTABLE DEVICES

Implantable devices require advanced technology in order to safely stay inside the body, and so have only been used since the 1950s. The first pacemaker was successfully implanted in 1958 (see page 18), and since then, numerous advances in science and engineering have allowed for the development and improvement of a whole range of devices. Today, it is thought that 6% of people in higher-income countries are fitted with implantables, which help to increase their quality of life and life expectancy.

While implantables are relatively modern, the science behind them has been known for hundreds of years. The Italian scientist Luigi Galvani is credited with discovering bioelectricity, the study of electrical signals that run through living organisms. In 1780, Galvani and his wife Lucia observed that when they passed an electrical current through a dead frog's legs, they were able to make them move. From this, they theorized that animal muscles were controlled by electricity. Galvani referred to this as "animal electricity," which today we call electrophysiology. Engineers today use the science behind electrophysiology to create modern implantable devices that replicate human biology.

Early pacemakers and cochlear implants required wires to transmit medical information to doctors, and had batteries that needed regular replacing. Modern pacemaker batteries can last as long as 10 years, and implants use new technologies such as Bluetooth® to share information wirelessly. This allows users to check their computers and mobile phones to monitor their health, and even receive warnings about any unusual signals.

3D printing has also revolutionized the world of medical implants, with tailor-made devices perfectly built to fit a wearer's body. This is becoming more common for hip, knee, and spine replacements.

ARNE LARSSON
The man with 27 hearts

In 1958, Swedish engineer Arne Larsson became ill with a viral infection that damaged the cells responsible for coordinating electrical signals around his heart. This meant that his heart didn't contract consistently or as much as it needed to, and put Larsson at risk of suffering harmful fainting episodes. His life was in danger. Larsson would have to be resuscitated up to 30 times a day, and live in constant fear of his heart potentially giving out, completely changing his lifestyle.

Larsson and his doctors knew a pacemaker (see pages 20–21) could help set the rhythm of his heart again, but the only versions available at the time were large, stationary machines, designed for temporary use in a single room. But thankfully, new implantable pacemakers were being developed at the same time. These devices used silicone transistors—a breakthrough piece of technology that made them small enough to remain inside their user's chest. All Larsson needed was a doctor who was willing to give the new pacemakers a try…

The initial operation was a success, but it didn't last long. After just eight hours, the device failed, and Larsson needed a backup fitted. The next operation was more successful and lasted eight years. Larsson would get a total of 26 pacemakers implanted over his lifetime, either to fix a broken one or to upgrade an existing one with new technology.

With his new and upgraded heart, Larsson lived until he was 86 and was able to return to his life as an electrical engineer. The 44 years he lived after his first operation would not have been possible without this triumph of medicine and technology, and millions of other pacemaker users are grateful for his bravery and pioneering steps.

HOW PACEMAKERS WORK

Pacemakers are small devices that monitor and regulate the electrical impulses controlling the heart. Normally, the heart regulates its own beating through a network of cells that carry electrical currents. These cells are coordinated by something called the sinoatrial node, which is often referred to as the "natural pacemaker." Medical conditions that affect the sinoatrial node, or any of the cells under its control, can be dangerous and require a pacemaker to correct them.

There are different types of pacemakers for different heart issues, but the basic idea behind them is the same. By sending electrical impulses only when irregular beats are detected, pacemakers mimic the role of the sinoatrial node and keep the heart functioning as it should.

Inside the pacemaker box

The battery lasts about six years. It gives plenty of warning when it is running low, and doctors monitor it closely.

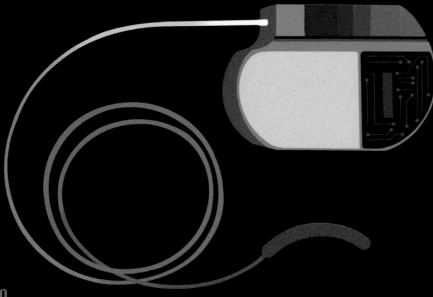

1. The pacemaker box (see opposite page) contains the battery and computer and sits inside the body between the heart and the left collarbone.

2. Thin wires called leads travel from the pacemaker box inside the body to the heart. Barbs at the end of the leads attach directly to the muscle and relay electrical information to the computer.

3. The computer detects, analyzes, and records information from the leads and sends electrical impulses of its own if the beating of the heart becomes abnormal.

EYEWEAR

Eyeglasses may seem commonplace today, but it has taken hundreds of years to develop them to where they are now, helped by a series of inventions along the way. The ancient Romans first wrote about using glass beads to read, similar to how reading glasses work today. However, it was the Arab scientist Al-Hasan Ibn al-Haytham, a man known as the "father of modern optics," who first wrote about using convex (outward curved) lenses to magnify an image. Eventually, Ibn al-Haytham's literature made its way to Western Europe, and translations of his work led to glass "reading stones" becoming common. The Italians improved further on these stones to create the first eyeglasses in the late 1200s.

New materials have allowed frames for glasses to become lighter and more durable. The color of lenses has changed too, creating the first purpose-built sunglasses. These work by adding cerium oxide (a type of chemical compound) into the glass to filter out harmful ultraviolet light from the sun. Sunglasses quickly became fashionable, and in 1938, it was reported that 20 million sunglasses had been sold the year before in the US. Interestingly, only a quarter of those people needed sunglasses for medical reasons. This development is an example of a product that was initially designed to benefit a few but ended up benefitting many. It is a testament to the importance of innovation within the disabled community.

The latest breakthrough in eyewear has come more recently, with EnChroma® glasses first launching in 2012. These special glasses are designed to help alleviate problems caused by color-blindness.

People who are color-blind find it difficult to distinguish between certain colors, such as red and green. EnChroma® glasses use the same principle as cerium oxide in the first sunglasses, but instead of filtering out harmful UV light, EnChroma® glasses filter out the wavelengths of light that get confused by the brain in those people with red-green color vision deficiency.

EYE REPLACEMENTS

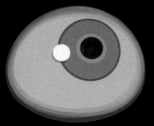

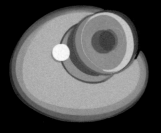

While glasses can be used to correct poor eyesight, historically fewer options were available to people who had lost their eye entirely. The first prosthetic eye dates from as early 2900 BCE and was found in Iran. It was sculpted using tar and animal fat, and decorated with gold, creating a surreal-looking object that sat inside the empty eye socket or in front of the damaged eye. This type of prosthesis certainly wouldn't have provided any function to its wearer, but would have been designed to be more aesthetically pleasing.

Over the next 5,000 years, the materials improved, but the lack of function remained the same. In the 1500s, glass blowers in Italy created realistic-looking glass eyes, and in the early 1900s, technology advanced to allow for the creation of lighter-weight synthetic materials such as porcelain and plastic. These advances were more comfortable and looked increasingly lifelike.

Bionic Eyes

The concept of a bionic eye has been around for as long as cameras have been around, but it wasn't until the 21st century that it was possible for scientists to make it a reality. First tested in 2006, the Argus II Retinal Prosthesis system is a prosthetic device that allows people with the disease retinitis pigmentosa to see again. People who live with the disease experience a breakdown in cells on the light-sensitive tissue at the back of the eye (the retina), causing loss of vision. Wearers of the Argus II are able to detect changes in light and motion, although they are not able to see color. This amazing piece of technology enables them to read text and recognize objects in their surroundings after losing their vision.

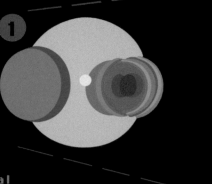

1. A short surgical procedure attaches an electronic device on the retina of a patient.

2. The user puts on a special pair of glasses with a camera at the front. This wirelessly sends signals to a portable processing unit.

3. The processing unit stimulates the retina with electrical signals. It is powered by a battery pack worn around the wearer's waist.

KEITH HAYMAN

"Having spent half my life in darkness, I can now tell when my grandchildren run towards me."

The first bionic eye in the UK was implanted in 2009, when British man Keith Hayman and others received the Argus II Bionic Eye as part of a clinical trial at the University of Manchester. Hayman used to work as a butcher, but he had been retired for over 25 years due to a condition called retinitis pigmentosa. This inherited condition caused him to lose his vision, and there had previously been no medicinal treatment or cure. One morning, Hayman's sister saw an advertisement on a local news channel, which was promoting clinical trials using a device that could restore vision for those living with retinitis pigmentosa. A few telephone calls and interviews later, and Hayman was selected to be part of the trial. He underwent a four-and-a-half-hour operation to have part of the device fitted to his retina.

When he was later asked about the decision to be part of the trial, Hayman said that he had nothing to lose and that "at worst, there would be no change; and at best, he would get some of his vision back." This courageous decision worked in his favor as after a few weeks of getting to know his new device, Hayman found himself seeing firework displays for the first time in a quarter of a century. The bionic eye did more than just allow Hayman to see—it allowed him to feel more independent. With the new device, he was able to walk into a shop and not be afraid of bumping into objects. He could even walk around in the dark without having to feel his way. Psychologically, the Argus II allowed Hayman to regain some of his confidence, and he no longer felt isolated. For Hayman, it felt important to be able to interact with the world with all his senses, and this device helped him to achieve that.

HOW COCHLEAR IMPLANTS WORK

Cochlear implants are tiny electronic devices that can treat hearing loss. They have a huge impact on the lives of those who use them. These small, complicated implants should not be confused with a hearing aid. Hearing aids act like little speakers, which make surrounding sounds louder so they can be heard by those whose ears aren't as sensitive as others. Cochlear implants directly transmit signals to the brain, which translates them into sounds.

Sound waves travel from the outer ear, through the middle ear, and into the inner ear. The cochlea is a fluid-filled chamber that sits inside the inner ear. In regular hearing, the movement of the fluid causes sensitive hair cells within the cochlea to bend. This generates an electrical signal that is sent to the brain. However, disease, damage, or deformity of the cochlea can send unclear signals to the brain, or no signal at all, causing hearing impairment or deafness. Cochlear implants can simulate the hearing process by carrying out the job of these malfunctioning parts.

Mayo Clinic was one of the first centers to use cochlear implants to treat kids with hearing loss caused by auditory neuropathy spectrum disorder. This disorder is responsible for up to 10 percent of hearing loss cases in babies with deafness caused by damage to the inner ear or the brain.

1.

A small microphone sits above the ear and detects the sounds all around.

2.

The microphone passes these sounds onto a speech processor, which filters the different sounds and selects which ones to pass on to the wearer to hear.

3.

The transmitter and stimulator pass these sounds from the processor, converting them into electrical signals.

4.

An electrode array, which sits inside the inner ear, collects these electrical signals and sends them into the auditory nerve, which passes them on to the brain.

BIONIC LIMBS

In order to create bionic limbs, scientists and engineers must first understand how human limbs work, and then try to replicate them. There are several different ways that bionic limbs can function. In this section, we understand how bionic limbs work, and the various ways they can be used.

Electrode Control

All muscle movements begin in the brain. The brain sends signals in the form of electrical impulses along nerves to the muscles they are trying to control. These impulses are interpreted by the muscle cells in the limb, and they tell the muscle to either contract or relax. This repeated and coordinated contracting and relaxing causes movement.

The process isn't too different when it comes to controlling bionic limbs. In fact, there is just one extra step. Movement still begins in the brain, but instead of the electrical impulses going directly to the limb they want to control, people who use bionic limbs send signals to electrodes instead, which sense muscle activity under the skin. The electrodes detect the electrical impulses and pass them onto a small computer, which translates the signals into movement. The more complicated the movement, the more electrodes are needed.

Body-Powered Control

Body-powered control is one of the oldest ways of controlling a prosthetic limb, and has been around since 1818, when the German dentist, Peter Bailiff, designed an upper limb prosthesis. This method of control has remained so popular because it is the simplest and requires the least technology. It is called "body-powered" because the limbs are controlled by other parts of the wearer's body. For example, movements in the arm and shoulder are detected by a harness, which moves a cable that opens and closes the hand. These prostheses therefore might not work for someone who is missing multiple limbs.

Limb Loss and Preservation Registry

In 2022, Mayo Clinic launched the Limb Loss and Preservation Registry, the first national database of its kind in the U.S. This registry aims to collect and track treatment outcomes to help experts determine which innovations are most helpful in treating those with limb differences or loss.

PROSTHETIC HANDS THROUGH THE AGES

Hands are one of our most valuable and versatile body parts. We use them to pick up objects, use tools, and feel textures, but also to communicate and bond with others through touch and expressive gestures. It comes as no surprise that humans have been desperate to replicate hands for those who were born without them, or lost them through accidents, injury, or disease. Because of the huge variety of tasks we use our hands for, this has been incredibly challenging, but it is fascinating to look back on over 500 years of advancement.

Early History

For almost as long as humans have roamed the Earth, there is evidence of tools being used as early prosthetic hands, including hooks, clamps, and knives, which were strapped to the body. These were limited to performing just one function and did not come close to the complexity of a human hand.

Götz von Berlichingen, 1500s

The most notable attempt to mimic nature was the iron arm worn by the German knight Götz von Berlichingen who lost his right hand in battle (see page 11). This advanced early prosthesis could bend at the knuckles, allowing Götz to hold the reins of a horse, or even a weapon. However, it was so heavy it would have needed to be strapped to his body.

Ambroise Paré, 1575

French military surgeon Ambroise Paré popularized amputations as a means to save a soldier's life on the battlefield. He drew designs of a spring-loaded hand that could be locked to hold an object. Early in the next century, prostheses began to be designed for everyday use.

Bowden Cable Control System, 1948

Both the First and Second World Wars resulted in a large increase in the population of people with arm amputations, so prosthetic hands began to receive more attention and investment. The first big success was the Bowden prosthesis, which was an affordable and reliable device that used cables to open and close a three-pronged hook. The cables were tied around the wearer's torso. Because of their simplicity and durability, these devices are still used around the world.

Myoelectric device, 1948

Myoelectric devices are the most common type of lower arm prosthesis today. Scientists developed them to introduce electrical signals to control the prosthetic hand more naturally. The first myoelectric device was invented by German physics student Reinhold Reiter and had motorized fingers. However, the device was bulky and couldn't be used for everyday situations. It wasn't until 1990 that myoelectric sensors were suitable for fitting inside prosthetic sockets.

i-LIMB®, 2008

Technology evolved to make prostheses, and the sockets they attach to, lighter, more durable, and more realistic. In 2008, tech company Touch Bionics released the i-LIMB®, the first prosthetic hand to have five independently powered digits that could bend at the joints. This revolutionary device became so successful because it accurately replicated human biology.

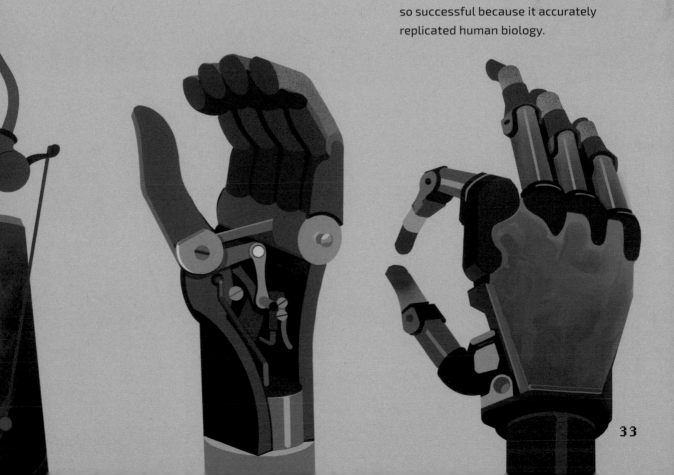

ROBERT CAMPBELL AIRD

"Part man, part machine, all Scottish."

In 1982, Edinburgh-born Robert Campbell Aird was diagnosed with cancer, and needed to have his right arm amputated to stop the disease from spreading further. Sixteen years after the surgery, Aird's life would change again.

In 1998, a team of five biomedical engineers created the world's first "Edinburgh Modular Arm System," otherwise known as a bionic arm. Though some prototypes existed already, this was the first bionic arm that was ready to be used outside of laboratory conditions. Aird became the first person in the world to use the revolutionary device. Under its super-realistic artificial skin lay advanced circuitry, microchips, gears, motors, and pulleys, enabling him to control his new arm. Just as a human arm might do, the bionic arm could rotate at the shoulder, bend at the elbow, twist at the wrist, and grip using fingers. With his new right arm, Aird was able to take a book from the bookshelf for the first time since his cancer treatment.

But it wasn't just picking up books that Aird was able to do. He certainly made the most of his restored ability, by taking flying lessons and even winning 14 trophies for clay pigeon shooting. Aird was a born adventurer. He believed that everything was a challenge, and nothing was impossible. He spent his free time working with biomedical engineers to improve the technology that he had benefitted from so much, and taking on charity work. Aird showed anything was possible when human and machine joined forces to make the most of life.

PROSTHETIC LEGS THROUGH THE AGES

Roman Empire, 300 BCE

The earliest example of a prosthetic leg is from ancient Rome, from around 300 BCE. The Capua leg had a wooden core surrounded by iron and bronze, with a hollow section at the top to attach to the wearer's leg. This type of prosthesis was rare, probably due to the need for bronze by the military.

Ambroise Paré, c.1579

Over the next 1,800 years, wooden peg legs were most commonly used, as they could be easily sourced and replaced, even if they weren't comfortable. But in 1579, French military surgeon Ambroise Paré released a book showing illustrations for a mechanical leg with a knee joint that could bend and lock into place.

Benjamin Palmer, 1846

Unlike the technology required for prosthetic hands, the advancement of prosthetic legs depended on new materials being discovered and made available. In 1846, amputee Benjamin Palmer's design for a prosthetic leg with a heel spring and metal tendons was patented. It attempted to replicate human joint movement.

Early prosthetic legs were crude, uncomfortable, and limited the wearer. However, an explosion of new technologies, materials, and knowledge in the 20th century led to some huge leaps forward. Newer synthetic materials, advanced technology, and custom fittings are making prosthetic devices stronger and increasingly versatile today.

Computer-Controlled Legs, 2000s

Icelandic orthopedic company Össur, and Professor Hugh Herr at the Massachusetts Institute of Technology (MIT), developed some of the first computer-controlled legs. These use sensors and microprocessors to detect changes in the environment and make minor adjustments. For example, the PROPRIO FOOT® can lift the toes up on every step, preventing trips and falls. The prosthetic sensors also detect changes in the gradient of a slope if the wearer is walking up or downhill, and alters the angle of the foot, exactly like a human ankle. The RHEO KNEE® uses similar technology so that wearers who are missing their knees can have their whole leg adapt to the ground they walk on.

Special Blades

For leisurely walking, not much energy is needed to push off the ground. But in order to run, the shape of the foot needs to be adjusted to allow the wearer to spring forward. Engineers working with flexible carbon fiber came up with the "C" shape design. These running "blades" were inspired by cheetahs' hind legs.

POWERED EXOSKELETONS AND SUITS

All the bionic devices mentioned in this book so far have been designed to replace a single body part or function. However, some people who have experienced spinal injuries are not able to use their bodies below where the injury occurred, affecting more than one body part. People with paralysis that affects the torso, arms, and legs are called quadriplegic. People who have lost the use of their legs are called paraplegic. In 1965, a prototype was released that revolutionized the world of bionics—the exoskeleton.

Up until then, the only way people with paraplegia could move around was using a wheelchair. In the 1960s, the industrial company General Electric released the prototype of an exoskeleton allowing paraplegics to do something previously thought impossible—to stand and walk of their own accord. The word "exoskeleton" means "outer skeleton" and it is a device worn outside the body. Unlike prostheses, exoskeletons are not designed to replace a body part, but to support muscles and bones. These types of devices are called orthoses. The Hardiman, completed in 1971, was the first attempt to create a powered exoskeleton which could move the wearer's limbs. Unfortunately, the device's movements were so unpredictable, it was never tested on humans. Despite this, it is still considered to have made engineering breakthroughs, and represented one of the first attempts to marry "human and machine."

Metal rods act as
bones outside the
body, which can bend
at the joints to mimic
the movement of our
skeletons.

Modern Exoskeletons

As technology progressed, powered orthoses started to become more of a reality. Today, they are light enough to walk on different types of terrain and some have batteries that can last for a whole day on a single charge. Their aim is to reduce musculoskeletal stress, discomfort, muscle activity, and movement energetics. In 2014, Professor Hugh Herr at MIT developed the first powered leg exoskeleton to increase walking speed at lesser effort.

As the technology improves, the British military are looking into exoskeletons to see if they can "upgrade" soldiers of the future to be able to run faster, jump higher, and lift heavier items than most humans could ever dream of.

The wearer is able
to control the
exoskeleton through
a control panel on
their arm.

NEURAL IMPLANTS

It has long been a dream of scientists to try to tap directly into the signals that originate in the brain and control any device attached to the body. With this knowledge, rather than teaching someone how to use a bionic arm with muscles in their forearm, a neural implant could interpret signals in their brain to control bionic devices directly.

In 2018, Mayo Clinic published a study that investigated electrical brain stimulation and memory enhancement. Since then, their researchers have been working on an implantable chip that monitors the brain's electrical activity and forecasts whether a lasting memory will be created.

Neural implants have already been used for bionic eye technology (see page 25), but inventors are just starting to explore what is possible beyond this. In 2021, the company Neuralink released a video of a monkey playing the video game Pong, purely with the power of thought. The signals were sent wirelessly by microchips implanted into the monkey's brain. Neuralink plans to use this technology to allow paralyzed users to operate smartphones with their brains far faster than someone ever could with their thumbs. While this is currently not ready to be used outside of laboratories, it represents one of the most exciting breakthroughs in modern bionic technology.

The potential applications of this technology are endless. Not only would neural implants allow bionic arms and legs to have the same dexterity as human limbs, but quadriplegics or people with head injuries could control their own limbs once again.

CLAIRE LOMAS

"When I focused on what was possible, rather than dwelling on what wasn't, my life started to change."

Claire Lomas was born in 1980 and made a career for herself as a chiropractor and a competitive horse rider. In 2007, she had an accident when her horse collided with a tree, causing a spinal cord injury that saw her lose the use of her legs. Lomas coped with her injuries by combining her love of sports with her new need for rehabilitation therapy. She built up her core strength by exercising at the gym, swimming, skiing, and even horse riding, so that she could use her new wheelchair to the best of its ability.

Throughout all these activities, Lomas focused on public fundraising events and campaigns to fund new equipment, and to support charities who researched spinal cord repair treatments. The most famous of her campaigns was in 2012, when she became the first person to finish the London Marathon using a ReWalk™ exoskeleton. This device, combined with crutches, allowed Lomas to walk the full 26 miles (42 km) and incredibly, raise more than $250,000.

The marathon took a total of 17 days, and the ReWalk™ suit she used combined with Lomas's "never say die" attitude made this feat of endurance possible. Speaking on her mental resilience in 2012, Lomas said "When I focused on what was possible, rather than dwelling on what wasn't, my life started to change," meaning outlook is everything when it comes to embracing challenges and using bionic technology. Lomas has also spoken of the importance of family, and how she has not faced these challenges alone, taking strength from the support of her husband and their two children.

THE PARALYMPICS

The advancements in prosthetic technology can be seen in action in the Paralympic Games. This sporting event brings together the finest athletes with disabilities from around the world, and has taken place every four years since 1960. While disabled sports competitions have been recorded as far back as the 1900s, the large numbers of injured veterans after the Second World War created an increase in disabled adults who used sports as part of their rehabilitation, while others used sports for fitness and leisure.

The Stoke Mandeville Hospital in the UK trialed using sports as a form of therapy. Dr Ludwig Guttmann organized a competition for wheelchair athletes from the hospital to compete in, arranging for it to occur on the opening day of the 1948 Olympic Games. Four years later, veterans from the Netherlands joined in, and they were called the International Stoke Mandeville Games. By 1960, more than 400 athletes from 23 nations competed in eight events, and they were renamed the Paralympic Games. *Para* is a Greek word meaning "alongside," to show the Games' connection to the Olympic Games.

Each year the Paralympic Games become bigger, both in terms of the number of athletes competing as well as the number of sports. In the Tokyo 2020 Paralympic Games, 4,403 athletes competed in 539 events in 22 different sports, with badminton and taekwondo becoming the latest additions. The athletes become ever more impressive.

Long Jump›

Specially adapted blades provide long jump athletes with a faster pace for the run-up and improved push-off to get the maximum distance out of a jump.

‹Taekwondo

There are two forms of taekwondo. Kyorugi (sparring) for athletes with limb impairments and Poomsae (martial art forms) for athletes with neurological impairments.

Palak Kohli >

Kohli is a rising star of Paralympic sports. She was born in 2002 without her left arm and became the youngest female Para-badminton player at the Tokyo Paralympics across three events: women's singles and doubles, as well as mixed doubles. By age 18, Kohli had already won 20 medals in tournaments across different competitions. Despite challenges, Kohli continues to speak positively of her disability, claiming it is her superpower.

Wakako Tsuchida ⌄

Tsuchida is a veteran athlete who has cemented her legacy as an icon of Paralympic sports. She was born in 1974 and lost both legs above the knee after a car accident in 1992. As part of her rehabilitation, Tsuchida took part in sports and quickly excelled in many areas. She is the first Japanese athlete to win medals at both the Summer and Winter Paralympic Games, as well as the first female captain for the Japanese Summer Paralympics. Incredibly, Tsuchida has competed in four Winter and three Summer Paralympic Games, with medals in ice sledge racing and wheelchair racing.

RICHARD WHITEHEAD

"When you fail, you learn a lot about yourself and come back stronger."

All sports offer a chance for heroes to be born. One such example is Richard Whitehead MBE, who was born in 1976 with a condition that meant that he had to have both of his legs amputated at the knees. Having lost two friends to bone cancer, Whitehead decided to raise money for charities that funded bone cancer research. His natural sportiness was evident, but Whitehead had never run more than a mile before, as he had never worn prostheses designed for running. Thirteen days before the marathon, orthopedic company Össur (see page 37) heard of his story and fitted Whitehead with his first running blades. He went on to complete the New York Marathon in 2004.

Whitehead's hunger to compete as an athlete grew, and he took part in his first international event at the 2006 Winter Paralympic Games. Though they were unsuccessful for him, Whitehead would go on to prove that "defeat always stimulates you to work harder," winning the gold medal in the T42 200m sprint in the London 2012 Paralympics in a world record time. He won gold again in the same race in Rio de Janeiro, Brazil, in 2016.

Whitehead also had success in marathon running. In 2010, he set a world record for a lower-limb amputee to run the marathon in a time of 2:42:52. Three years later, he ran 40 marathons in 40 days to raise money for charity. This phenomenal feat of grit and determination proved the nickname, Lionheart, given to him by his grandmother when he was a child, to be the perfect way of describing him.

Whitehead has not only inspired the next generation of Paralympians, but his charitable work and attitude toward adversity has shown everyone what can be achieved when you put your mind to it.

THE CYBATHLON

As technology evolved, Paralympic organizers put a law in place stating that athletes could only use unpowered prostheses, so their performance would be based on physical ability and not the technology itself. However, as technological advancements became more exciting, both the wearers and the engineers who created them became keen to show off their inventions, and so, a new event was born.

In 2016, the Swiss Federal Institute of Technology in Zurich organized the Cybathlon —the first international competition to pit people and their advanced bionic limbs against each other on a series of everyday tasks. Every team is composed of a "pilot" (a disabled person who uses the technology) and their "technology provider" (usually a university or private company), and currently there are six disciplines they compete in.

Brain-Computer Interface Race

Pilots who are paralyzed from the neck down use brain-computer interfaces to control avatars in a computer game.

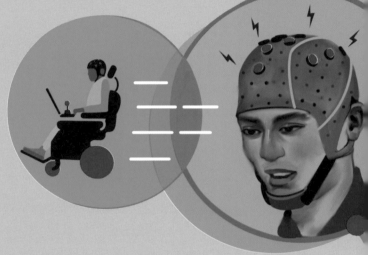

Powered Wheelchair Race

Pilots use their wheelchairs to overcome an obstacle course representing traditionally difficult tasks, such as walking up and down stairs.

Functional Electrical Stimulation Bike Race

Pilots who are paralyzed from the waist down send external signals to make their legs contract and ride a bike.

The Cybathlon has a dual purpose. Not only does it allow pilots to compete against each other, but it aims to promote conversations and create awareness about the new technologies that exist. The Cybathlon also aims to occur every four years, at the same time as the Olympic and Paralympic Games. While it is currently much smaller than the other events, the future is exciting. It will no doubt attract larger crowds, particularly if the technology surpasses what humans are able to do. Would you rather watch someone run 100m in 10 seconds or 5 seconds?

Powered Leg Prosthesis Race

Pilots with prosthetic legs race to complete some leg-based tasks as quickly as possible. These include walking up or down stairs, getting up from a chair, or walking across a beam.

Powered Arm Prosthesis Race

Using prosthetic hands, pilots hurry to complete daily tasks, such as tying shoelaces and zipping up a jacket as quickly as possible.

Powered Exoskeleton Race

Pilots use exoskeletons to race around an obstacle course, testing the ability of their suits.

BLAKE LEEPER

"Life is 10% what you deal with and 90% how you deal with it."

Remarkable American Paralympic athlete Blake Leeper was born in 1989 with both of his legs missing below the knee. Leeper's father was a coach, so he grew up with a natural affinity for sports. Leeper wanted to pursue a career in athletics from a young age, despite being told that he "wouldn't be able to run and jump like the rest of the kids."

Thankfully for Leeper, his hard work and determination paid off, and he made his debut for the US athletics team in 2009. Since 2011, Leeper has won a phenomenal eight Paralympic Track and Field medals for his country, and even set a world record in the 4x100m relay in 2013. His impressive accomplishments meant that in 2017, Leeper became the first double-leg amputee to compete against able-bodied Olympic athletes at the US Track & Field Championships.

Sadly, Leeper's career since has been surrounded by controversy. In 2020, the Court Arbitration for Sport (CAS) ruled that Leeper's running blades made him several inches taller than if he were able-bodied, giving him an unfair advantage. However, this ruling has been considered controversial, as the outcome was calculated using the Maximum Allowable Standing Height (MASH) measurement. This approach uses standards based on body proportions that Leeper's legal team argue is not racially inclusive. Leeper, who is African American, disputed that these standards do not represent his natural body proportions, and that the MASH system bases its height calculations on outdated photographs from a skewed sample population.

Leeper's appeal was denied, but his story is not the end of the road. Some people believe that it shows great progress to see able-bodied athletes contest that people without legs have an unfair advantage. Unfortunately, this case also serves as a reminder that there are many issues to solve and a long way to go.

BEYOND BIONICS

So far, bionic devices have been playing catch-up with the body parts they are trying to emulate. While the devices available today have changed lives, they are still not as multi-functional, reliable, and efficient as the organs and limbs that biology has provided. As we look at the rapid advancements that have been made since the start of the last century, we can be certain that technology will improve. However, instead of asking how we can replace an arm, leg, or eye, the question engineers ask today is: "how can we improve upon what an arm, leg, or eye is?"

Science and technology will continue to provide new options that are less expensive, more durable, and better at copying what humans can do. But there may come a point where we will ask what exactly makes a "good" limb. For example, a bionic arm is currently slower and less versatile than a human one. It needs to be charged and can't be submerged under water. But already bionic hands can hold onto objects that are very hot or cold without damaging themselves, which human hands cannot. A human leg can position itself on uneven ground without needing to go for maintenance, but running prostheses of the future may allow humans to run far quicker than biology ever could. There is no need to stop there—the fastest prosthetic leg of the future could even have wheels and an engine.

As technology continues to challenge
what is possible, it is the human brain that
will become the limiting factor. Where
do we stop? Is there a limit? Different
prostheses for specific tasks may become
as commonplace as changing into running
shoes or putting on scuba-diving equipment.

Looking further ahead, it could be possible
to replace all of our body parts with bionics.
Neurons in the brain could become fiber-
optic cables and muscles could be replaced
with synthetic fibers capable of moving
faster than a biological muscle. The difficult
question we would then face is what that
means for being human, and that,
no one yet has an answer to.

IMPLANTABLE ELECTRONIC CHIPS

Bionic innovations to date are designed to replace specific body functions that have been lost or damaged. But we have also begun to ask what we can *add* to our existing bodies. We are already experimenting with this idea through some of the technology we use every day—ear buds that sit inside our ears, and smartwatches wrapped around our wrists, for example—but the next step could be to literally get under our skin.

Implantable electronic chips are electronic circuit boards that are about the size of a grain of rice, or even smaller, and can be injected under the skin. They have been used since the 1980s to track and identify wild animals, but in recent years people have been implanting them into themselves for more complex tasks. The most common devices are microchips that are radio-frequency identification (RFID) implants, which are used to wirelessly communicate with other devices. RFID technology is already widely used for contactless card payments. People with RFID implants can use them to pay for goods and services, unlock doors, and store information, just as they would with a mobile phone. British scientist Kevin Warwick was the first person to do this in 1998.

Inviting this kind of technology inside our bodies is not without its downsides. As with any medical procedure, there is the risk of infection. But as well as human infections, implants also open up the possibility of catching computer viruses. In 2009, British scientist Mark Gasson had an RFID microchip implanted into his hand, which allowed him to enter a building. One month after the microchip was implanted, he and his team deliberately infected his implant with a computer virus, to prove that viruses could be transmitted to other systems and highlight the dangers. In doing so, Gasson became the first human to be infected with a computer virus. Though he experienced no side effects, he predicts he will not be the last.

While the applications of microchips are currently limited to a few simple functions, it is only a matter of time before their full potential is explored. Microchips have been suggested as an effective way of making sure athletes are locatable for drug testing, and if they become more widespread, microchips may even become important identification tools to help solve crime. However, these intrusive implants are seen by many as an invasion of privacy and may even be susceptible to data breaches, which poses many challenges.

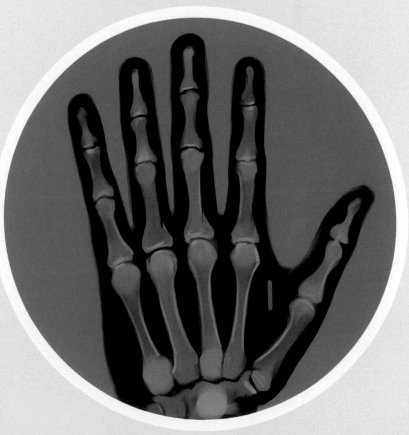

CYBORGS

If implantable electronic chips are the beginning of true integration between humans and machines, then cyborgs are the end goal. The word itself is a combination of the words "cybernetic" and "organism," and it means "a living thing with both organic and synthetic parts that communicate in both directions with each other." Cyborgs were historically futuristic organisms that belonged to science fiction, but technology exists today that proves they are no longer confined to stories.

Scientific engineering has reached an important milestone. Today, not only are engineers capable of creating prosthetic limbs to replace biological limbs, but they can create new limbs entirely. We can dream up new human parts that have never existed before and connect them to our brains. This new era of prostheses will bring about full integration between humankind and machines. In other words, we are becoming cyborgs.

The K. Lisa Yang Center for Bionics

Professor Hugh Herr is the co-director of the Yang Center for Bionics at MIT (see page 37). Dubbed the "leader of the bionic age," Herr has devoted his life's work to improving technological and human success, and creates the most advanced bionic limbs in the world.

The devices created at the Yang Center for Bionics are designed to wire directly into the wearer's biology, so that they can be controlled by remaining muscles and nerves from the brain, while also allowing anyone who wears these prostheses to "feel" them, just like a human limb.

But that is not all that is being developed here. The team is also designing limbs that do not exist in current biology. From extra arms to new exoskeletons and even wings, it may be possible for humans to add tools to themselves to become "superhumans."

While this technology is still in its early stages, Herr believes that humans will one day be able to do things that were previously thought impossible. Humans of the future may be unrecognizable in form and function from us today, and could completely change how we currently perceive limitation, intelligence, and expression of identity. This is a huge step into the future.

NEIL HARBISSON

"The biggest challenge for cyborgs is to be socially accepted."

Neil Harbisson was born in 1984 with achromatopsia, a condition that means he only sees black, white, and shades of grey. This gave him a unique perspective on his environment, and he found himself drawn to music and art from a young age.

In 2004, Harbisson had a prosthetic antenna implanted into the occipital bone at the back of his skull. The antenna has a camera on one end and a sound vibration implant on the other. When the antenna's camera detects any changes in electromagnetic (EM) radiation, it causes the implant to vibrate and, incredibly, allows Harbisson to "hear" different colors. This technology has informed every aspect of his life, from the clothes he wears to the food he eats.

Because the camera detects EM radiation and not just color, Harbisson can also experience colors that human eyes cannot see by tapping into infrared and ultraviolet frequencies. This extra organ also allows Harbisson to create artworks that reflect what he experiences. Referred to as "cyborg art," he describes his approach as similar to sculpture-making, except he is molding his mind to create interesting and beautiful perceptions of reality. And he has not stopped there. Harbisson and his co-founder of the Cyborg Foundation, Moon Ribas, have both had two teeth replaced in their mouths. One is a button connected to Bluetooth technology, and the other is a vibrator. If one of them presses the button, it vibrates the other tooth, and allows the two of them to communicate via Morse code.

These examples are just the tip of the iceberg when it comes to the potential of cyborgs. As technology grows, we will become better at integrating it into our own bodies, and the possibilities of that are limitless.

RISKS AND REWARDS

There has never been a more exciting time to need a bionic upgrade. Whether eyes, ears, arms, legs, or even the whole body, options exist today that have the power to truly change lives. But as science evolves ever faster and further, the most important question we now have to face is, "How far are we willing to go?."

In the case of people who have lost function due to illness or an accident, bionics represent a chance to regain what they once had. In this scenario, bionics can be empowering and the most advanced technology should be available to all who need it. But as engineers create limbs and organs that exceed what human bodies are naturally capable of, we may find that people without disabilities will choose bionic organs and limbs over the ones they were born with. Some see this as a frightening point in our evolution. What will happen to the human race if we begin creating "superhumans," who are faster, stronger, and smarter? Is it inevitable that technology will surpass our biology?

But to see the other side to this, we must look even further ahead. Humans have always been explorers and dreamers. For as long as we have walked the Earth, we have looked toward the stars and wondered what is out there. Our species has developed some incredible technology and we are advancing every day. These developments may allow us to one day travel across space and finally get the answers to questions our ancestors could only dream of. For this to become a reality, we must keep experimenting as we always have done, while never losing sight of what makes us human. As Human 2.0s, let us continue to evolve together.

"Imagination is more important than knowledge. For knowledge is limited, whereas imagination embraces the entire world, stimulating progress, giving birth to evolution."

Albert Einstein, 1931

ABOUT THE AUTHOR

Patrick Kane is a writer, motivational speaker, campaigner, and Ambassador to The UK Sepsis Trust. In 1998, he became a triple amputee after contracting meningococcal septicemia as a 9-month-old baby. In 2010, he became the then-youngest person in the world to be fitted with a revolutionary bionic arm. Since then, he was chosen to carry the Olympic Torch as part of the London 2012 Olympic Games, spoken at TEDxTeen in 2014, written numerous articles on the changing role of disability with technology, appeared at Apple's 2014 World Wide Developer's Conference and at WIRED: Next Generation in 2015. In 2020, Patrick graduated from the University of Edinburgh with a degree in Biochemistry.

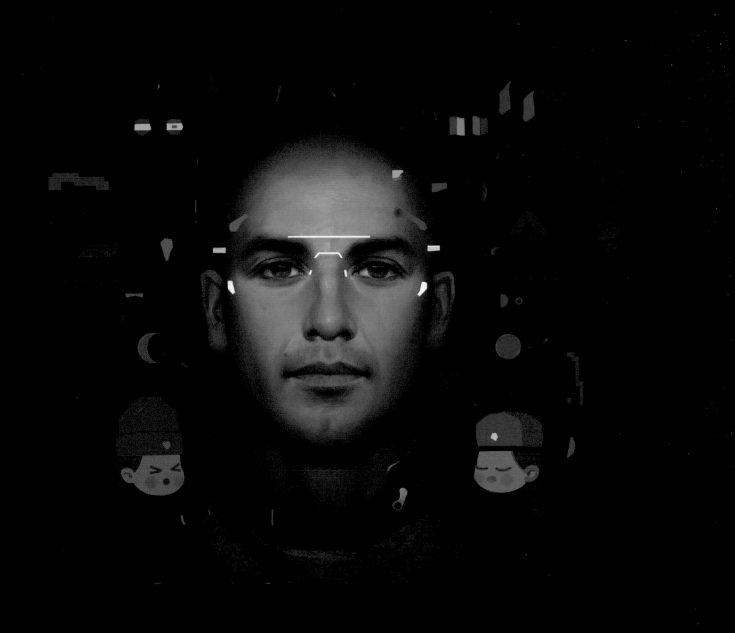

ABOUT THE ARTIST

Samuel Rodriguez is based out of San José, California, and has had his work shown in public art spaces, museums, companies, galleries, and editorial publications. He started out as a graffiti artist and later decided to change direction and pursue a Bachelor in Fine Arts at The California College of the Arts. Rodriguez has since blended what he absorbed from past experiences to create his current style. His work is heavily motivated by his interest in social, historical, and cultural hybridity.

TIMELINE

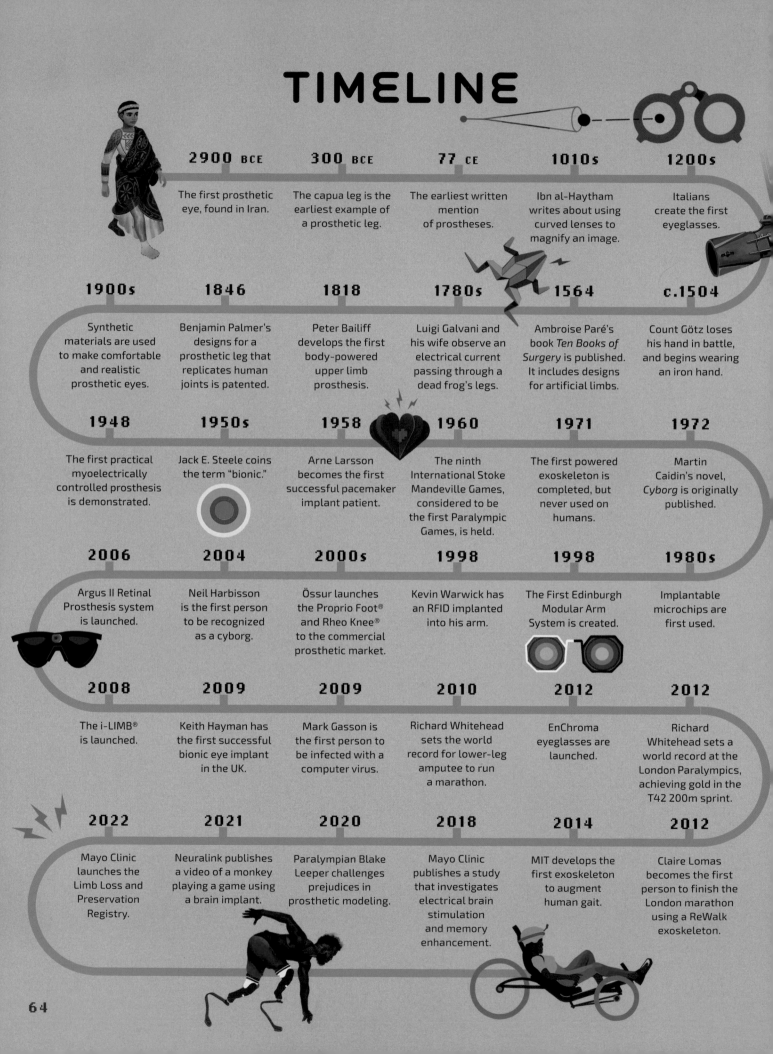

2900 BCE
The first prosthetic eye, found in Iran.

300 BCE
The capua leg is the earliest example of a prosthetic leg.

77 CE
The earliest written mention of prostheses.

1010s
Ibn al-Haytham writes about using curved lenses to magnify an image.

1200s
Italians create the first eyeglasses.

1900s
Synthetic materials are used to make comfortable and realistic prosthetic eyes.

1846
Benjamin Palmer's designs for a prosthetic leg that replicates human joints is patented.

1818
Peter Bailiff develops the first body-powered upper limb prosthesis.

1780s
Luigi Galvani and his wife observe an electrical current passing through a dead frog's legs.

1564
Ambroise Paré's book *Ten Books of Surgery* is published. It includes designs for artificial limbs.

c.1504
Count Götz loses his hand in battle, and begins wearing an iron hand.

1948
The first practical myoelectrically controlled prosthesis is demonstrated.

1950s
Jack E. Steele coins the term "bionic."

1958
Arne Larsson becomes the first successful pacemaker implant patient.

1960
The ninth International Stoke Mandeville Games, considered to be the first Paralympic Games, is held.

1971
The first powered exoskeleton is completed, but never used on humans.

1972
Martin Caidin's novel, *Cyborg* is originally published.

2006
Argus II Retinal Prosthesis system is launched.

2004
Neil Harbisson is the first person to be recognized as a cyborg.

2000s
Össur launches the Proprio Foot® and Rheo Knee® to the commercial prosthetic market.

1998
Kevin Warwick has an RFID implanted into his arm.

1998
The First Edinburgh Modular Arm System is created.

1980s
Implantable microchips are first used.

2008
The i-LIMB® is launched.

2009
Keith Hayman has the first successful bionic eye implant in the UK.

2009
Mark Gasson is the first person to be infected with a computer virus.

2010
Richard Whitehead sets the world record for lower-leg amputee to run a marathon.

2012
EnChroma eyeglasses are launched.

2012
Richard Whitehead sets a world record at the London Paralympics, achieving gold in the T42 200m sprint.

2022
Mayo Clinic launches the Limb Loss and Preservation Registry.

2021
Neuralink publishes a video of a monkey playing a game using a brain implant.

2020
Paralympian Blake Leeper challenges prejudices in prosthetic modeling.

2018
Mayo Clinic publishes a study that investigates electrical brain stimulation and memory enhancement.

2014
MIT develops the first exoskeleton to augment human gait.

2012
Claire Lomas becomes the first person to finish the London marathon using a ReWalk exoskeleton.